GW00578221

Vía Lucis

The Way of the Resurrection

By David O'Malley SDB

Christ is the Lord of a history that moves.
He not only holds the beginning and the end in his hands.
But he is history with us, walking ahead of us to where we are going.
He is not always in the same place.

Thomas Merton

ISBN 0-9538991-8-7
Don Bosco Publications
Thornleigh House
Bolton BL1 6PQ
Tel 01204 308 811

Printed by Printoff Graphic Arts Ltd

CONTENTS

INTRODUCTION

In addition to the engaging liturgies of the Easter *Triduum*, the Way of the Cross was a popular devotion which thrived throughout the Second Millennium of Christianity. Sometimes referred to by its Latin name, *Via Crucis*, it was followed, usually on Fridays, during the Forty Days of Lent. The *Via Lucis, the Way of Light*, emerges from the resurrection stories in the same spirit of devotion.

The *Via Lucis* is particularly suited for Easter Sunday, for the weekdays of Easter, and throughout the Easter Season.

In a fashion similar to the Way of the Cross, the *Via Lucis* reflects upon the final chapters of each of the four gospels, which narrate the appearances of the Risen Lord from Easter to Pentecost. Fourteen *Stations of Light* have been identified.

The official Vatican prayer book for the Jubilee Year 2000, *Pilgrim Prayers*, includes a *Via Lucis* alongside the traditional stations of the cross. It is hoped that this book will help the Christian community, which has so passionately identified with the Crucified Lord on the way of the cross, move from the darkness of the Easter tomb towards the light of the Spirit at Pentecost. In looking at their own experience they may discover the spirit that gives them new reasons for living and hoping.

LETTING GO

The First Station

Jesus is Risen

Luke 24: 1 – 9, 11

On the first day of the week, at the first sign of dawn, they went to the tomb with the spices they had prepared. They found that the stone had been rolled away from the tomb, but on entering discovered that the body of the Lord Jesus was not there. As they stood there, not knowing what to think, two men in brilliant clothes suddenly appeared at their side. Terrified, the women lowered their eyes. But the two men said to them,

> *'Why look among the dead for someone who is alive? He is not here, he has risen. Remember what he told you when he was still in Galilee: that the Son of Man had to be handed into the power of sinful men and be crucified, and rise again on the third day.'*

And they remembered his words.

When the women returned from the tomb they told this to the eleven and to all the others. The other women with them also told the apostles, but this story of theirs seemed pure nonsense, and they did not believe them.

Life Experience

It was a significant moment and I felt myself slowing down to do this ordinary thing for the last time. We were clearing out our desks. It was the end of term, but for me it was the end of my time at college. I found myself lingering as I collected together the dusty bits and pieces of the years; broken pens, odd notes that had been passed during teaching sessions. My fingers found themselves touching the graffiti that covered the inside of the desk drawer, seeing it as if for the first time as well as the last.

In many ways I was glad to be moving on and letting go. Part of me felt a huge warmth for this room; for the memories it triggered, the experiences it held, and the friendships and battles it had witnessed over the years. Amidst all the noise and activity I found myself sat down again, my mind running in reverse and collecting the memories that seemed significant before I walked out into something totally new.

It was here, at this desk that I arranged my first date. This was the room in which I had struggled with French tests, and eventually admitted that I would never be as good as my sister. This was the place where I had my most embarrassing moment, one that I still shudder to remember.

This was the room where my favourite teacher had to tell me my Gran had died. So much of my life seemed to have taken place around this desk and these people. Now it was ending. It was right to stop for a while and reverence this moment, put my head down on the desk for one last time, and give thanks for it all, and ask God to sort out what was still confusing.

Life

Experience

Scriptural Meditation

Our lives are stitched together with a series of small beginnings and endings. There are many first times and last times that mark our progress through life. Some of them seem to stand out as times for stopping, recognising the moment and perhaps giving thanks. The women who took perfume to anoint Jesus' body and the young person in the classroom are doing similar things; they are recognising an ending and reverencing the moment. Slowing down activity, and coming to terms with all that has happened, is essential if we are to grow in wisdom and let life teach us. These moments are times to gather up what the past has to offer, but they are not times to cling onto for very long. The angels in the story remind the women not to look for too long at what is dead and what is done. Instead to look for life and God's presence in what is happening, in the present moment. That movement from death to life can be hard to make. It can be so easy to be trapped in our sadness and regret. All of us need to pause, and listen for the encouragement of angel voices to move us, forward into life.

The cult of the Holy Sepulchre is Christian only in so far
As it is the cult of a place where Christ is no longer to be found.
But such a cult can only be valid on one condition:
That we are willing to move on,
To follow him to where we are not yet,
To seek him where he goes before us - to Galilee.

Thomas Merton

Personal Reflection

In what ways am I still trapped in the past?

Where are the angel voices that call me back to life?

Prayer

Lord, help me to face the past honestly and not be swallowed up by it. Help me to move out of the tombs of past failures and disappointments, so that I can meet you in the challenge of living in the present moment. Show me how to echo the words of the angels at the tomb, so that those around me will be able to meet you, their risen Lord, in the days that lie ahead.

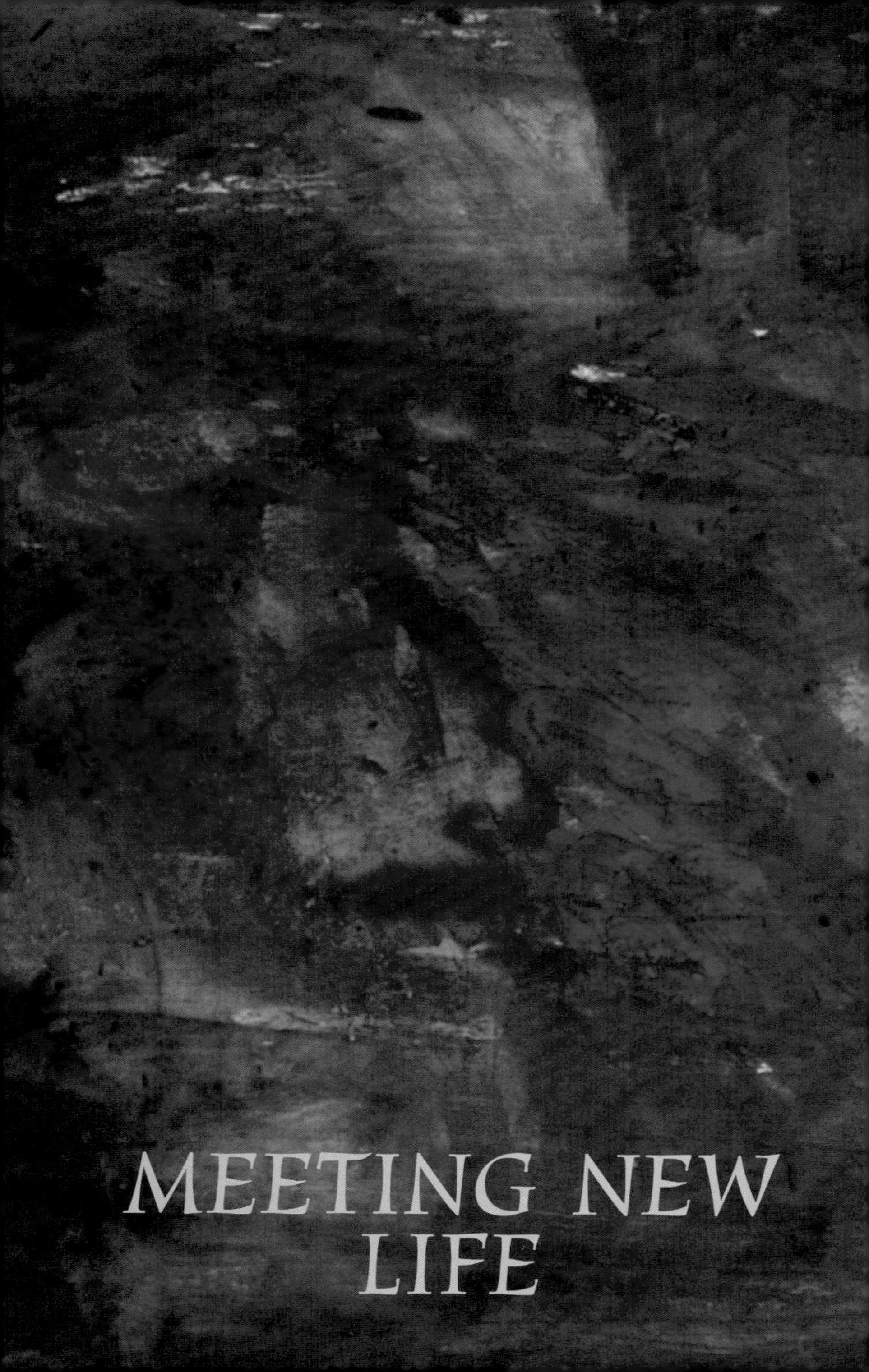

MEETING NEW LIFE

The Second Station

Peter and the other disciple run to the tomb

John 20: 3 - 9

So Peter set out with the other disciple to go to the tomb. They ran together, but the other disciple, running faster than Peter, reached the tomb first; he bent down and saw the linen cloths lying on the ground, but did not go in. Simon Peter who was following now came up, went right into the tomb, saw the linen cloths on the ground, and also the cloth that had been over his head; this was not with the linen cloths but rolled up in a place by itself. Then the other disciple who had reached the tomb first also went in; he saw and he believed.

Life Experience

My brother John was always the sporty one, never short of admirers and yet he just hasn't coped with moving house and school. I was amazed at how he seemed to fall apart without his normal circle of friends. His normal cheerfulness had left him, he was moody and seemed to lose all confidence. Getting started at the new school seemed to make things worse. He was always comparing everything to the old school. He didn't even want to be on the football team or sign on for the trips in the first term. I liked the old school well enough but I could see its faults too. I suppose being a bit older than John helps.

Perhaps I've got a stronger faith in myself and my gifts, and I am probably more realistic about how long it takes to adapt to a new situation.

Maybe it's just age then, or maybe it's that John is more outgoing whereas I'm more shy and quiet. Whatever the cause is, we certainly handle change very differently. It is frustrating to watch him struggling and not being able to help, he gets angry and upset easily and there's more tension in the house when he's around.

On the other hand there are times when we talk, like we have never talked before, and I can be his big brother. In spite of everything this move has brought John and me closer together and that feels brilliant.

Life

Experience

Scriptural Meditation

In the race to get to the tomb Peter was always going to lose. The other disciple, John, was young and fit. The middle-aged Peter must have struggled to even keep him in sight. It was good then that John waited and let Peter go inside the tomb first. It was Peter who saw that the tomb was tidy and the cloths folded up. Peter realised that he was not looking at a grave robbery but an event that was meant to be. Somehow all that Jesus had said must have dropped into place. Only then did John go in and they must have talked together. When we meet setbacks one of the most frustrating things is that we all do it in different ways. Some need to see and touch the situation. Others need to throw themselves into activity like John, sprinting ahead. Others seem to draw into themselves and find a way forward in their own hearts. All these ways have their place in meeting change and the new life of resurrection. The trouble is that we tend to get through them in our own way, and at our own pace. Like John and Peter we need patience, to wait for people. We need to believe in the new life and light that follows setbacks and change. The way that Peter saw and believed was a gift he was given, so that he could strengthen the faith of the others. Most of us have to struggle for that light to grow strong inside, and respect the way that light is growing in those around us.

Patience is needed with everyone, but first of all with ourselves

St Francis of Sales

Personal Reflection

How do I deal with setbacks and sadness?

Do I keep busy, go quiet, or need to talk things over again and again?

How do others around me deal with moving from sadness and loss towards light and hope?

Prayer

Lord, when things come to an end, it is not easy to see much good coming out of it. Sometimes, like Peter, we just need to see and believe and struggle. Let me use it as a doorway to deeper trust and faith in you. Help me to be patient with those who deal with the challenge of new beginnings in different ways from me. Help me wait for them, to recognise resurrection in their own lives with patience and faith.

Amen

COPING WITH GOOD NEWS

The Third Station

Jesus appears to Mary of Magdala

John 20: 11 – 17

Meanwhile Mary stayed outside near the tomb, weeping. Then, still weeping, she stooped to look inside, and saw two angels in white sitting where the body of Jesus had been, one at the head, the other at the feet. They said, 'Woman, why are you weeping?' 'They have taken my Lord away' she replied 'and I don't know where they have put him.' As she said this she turned round and saw Jesus standing there, though she did not recognise him. Jesus said, 'Woman, why are you weeping? Who are you looking for?' Supposing him to be the gardener, she said, 'Sir, if you have taken him away, tell me where you have put him, and I will go and remove him'. Jesus said, 'Mary!' She knew him then and said to him in Hebrew, 'Rabbuni!' - which means Master. Jesus said to her, 'Do not cling to me, because I have not yet ascended to the Father. but go and find the brothers, and tell them: I am ascending to my Father and your Father, to my God and your God.'

Life Experience

"The test results are clear." I felt the breath being sucked out of me as a wave of emotion swept back and spilled out in tears. I had armed myself against bad news and was unprepared for good news. I fell apart. The doctor said, "Anne, it's all OK you're going to be fine!" His voice seemed to come from miles away but also from within me too. He came around the desk, and I found myself hanging on to him and tears stained his light grey suit.

Gently he pushed me to arm's length. He looked at me. I must have seemed a real mess. "You need to look after yourself." he said. "You've had a shock. You have got your life back and a future, now you need to think what you're going to do."

He was absolutely right. I'd almost made my last will. I'd finished my job since I'd been ill. All my relationships had changed and I'd found real friendship in my family that I'd never dreamt possible. But now I was in bits, as weak as a baby. I just wanted to cling to someone and be held. I had to get a taxi home I was in such a state.

The next few days were just a series of tidal waves of tears and confused joy. I felt the energy of life and the future coming back, but it was too powerful and confusing. The need to be touched, to reconnect with life and people was almost unbearable.

Life

Experience

Scriptural Meditation

Sometimes good news seems unbelievable and sweeps us off our feet. We prepare ourselves for the worst. Like Mary we look towards the tomb, our eyes are too full of grief to see the possibility of a new future. In order to defend ourselves against disappointment we entertain disaster, and allow it a centre-stage position in our mind and heart. When we meet the risen Jesus it can disturb the tragic script we have written for ourselves. Like Mary we have to tear it up.

The confusion that comes with hope is a moment of grace, an opportunity to meet Jesus without a script, to renew and deepen our relationship with Him. But it is a moment that brings a fragile newness that needs protection and reflection. There is often a tendency to cling to what was, to slip into the familiar that has now changed forever.

These moments can take the form of dramatic life and death events, but they also happen to us each time we meet with any change and have to adapt. Every loss triggers a change that opens up new opportunities and challenges. Everything becomes grist to God's mill when we recognise that creation and each person is caught up into a process of dying and rising. Every morning can be a bleary-eyed resurrection, as we turn away from the dead hand of the past and begin life again in the company of the Risen Lord.

In the midst of winter I discovered within me an invincible summer.

Albert Camus

Personal Reflection

How do I cope with good news and surprises?

What do I notice first when things change, problems or possibilities?

Prayer

Lord, they call you the God of surprises, the one who can change death into new life. Help me to recognise the small surprising resurrection moments scattered through each day, as well as those dramatic moments when life turns me upside down. Show me how to cherish those moments of newness. May I not cling to the past when you call me into change. Help me to be evermore alive and become good news for those I live with.

AMEN

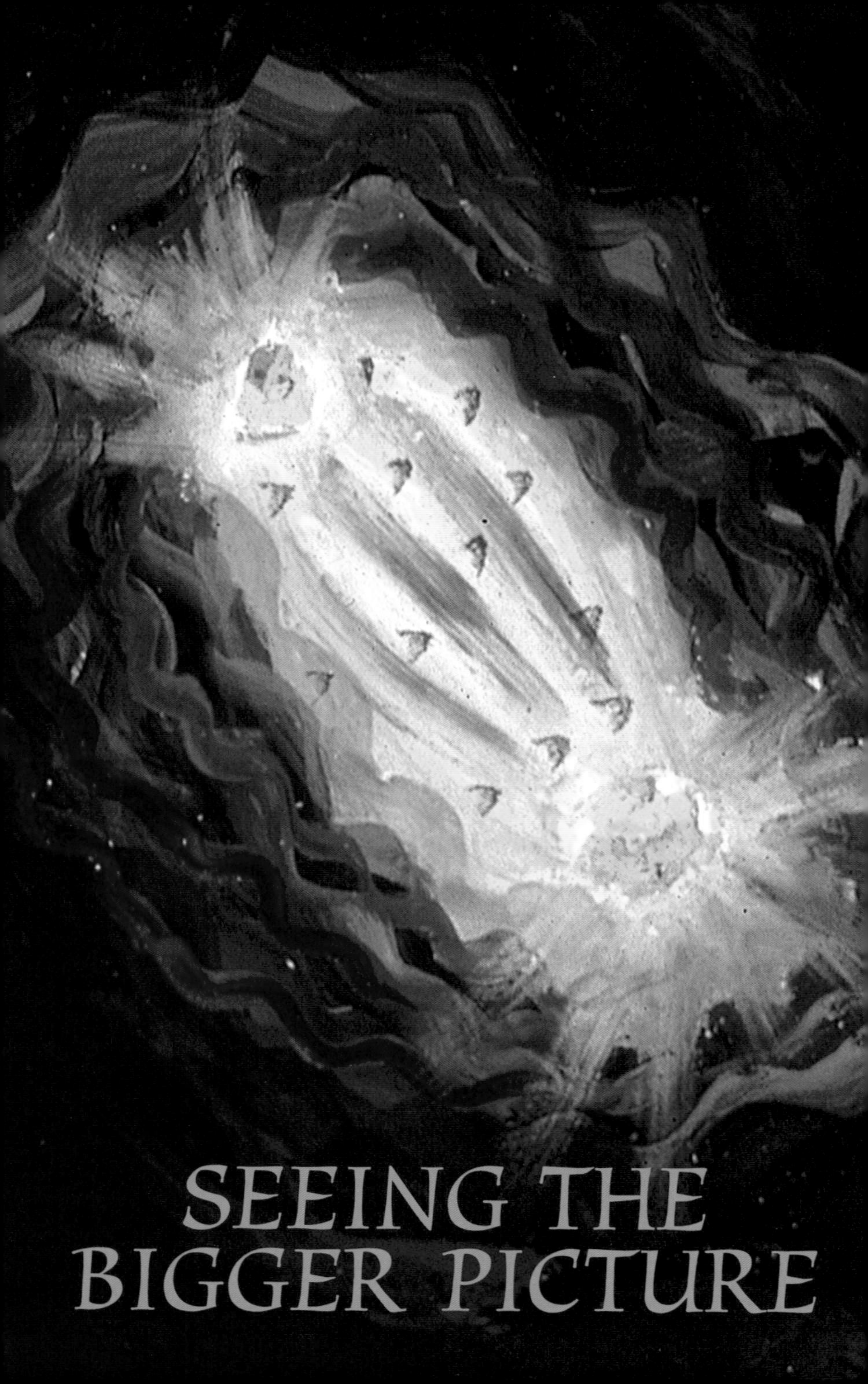
SEEING THE
BIGGER PICTURE

The Fourth Station

On the road to Emmaus

Luke 24: 13 - 19, 21 – 23, 25 - 27

That very same day, two of them were on their way to a village called Emmaus, seven miles from Jerusalem, and they were talking together about all that had happened. Now as they talked this over, Jesus himself came up and walked by their side; but something prevented them from recognising him. He said to them, 'What matters are you discussing as you walk along?' They stopped short, their faces downcast.

Then one of them, called Cleopas, answered him, 'You must be the only person staying in Jerusalem who does not know the things that have been happening there these last few days'. 'What things?' he asked. 'All about Jesus of Nazareth' they answered. 'Our own hope had been that he would be the one to set Israel free. And this is not all: two whole days have gone by since it all happened; and some women from our group have astounded us: they went to the tomb in the early morning, and when they did not find the body, they came back to tell us they had seen a vision of angels who declared he was alive.'

Then he said to them, 'You foolish men! So slow to believe the full message of the prophets! Was it not ordained that the Christ should suffer and so enter into his glory?' Then, starting with Moses and going through all the prophets, he explained to them the passages throughout the scriptures that were about himself.

Life Experience

I should have reserved a seat. The train was crammed with people. I decided to avoid the football fans and headed for the back of the train. It wasn't until I reached the smoking carriage that I found an empty seat and sunk gratefully into it. "You look all in," a voice said by my side. Oh no! I thought to myself. I'm sitting next to a talker, that's all I need! I said something non-committal and pulled out my novel, only to realise that he was reading the same novel. "Snap!" he said.

From that moment I began a conversation that changed my life. It started with talking just about the characters in the novel. Then somehow I slipped into talking about myself and the family problem I was on my way to sort out.

Each time I spoke about my disappointment he seemed to be able to flip it over into gratitude with just a word. Each time I spoke about a problem he recognised the challenge and the richness that could come from it. Yet he always heard what I was saying, and appreciated the struggle I was going through. At the end of the journey I wanted to keep talking, and hearing what he had to say. He seemed to see things in a totally different way.

Hearing him talk lit up my life in a way I'd never experienced. There was so much energy in me after the conversation that I actually felt enthusiasm, and a sense of privilege in facing the family problem I had dreaded. I wanted to ask him to stay a bit longer, but he had disappeared into the crowd leaving me with more strength and a huge amount of gratitude for the talk we had shared.

Life

Experience

Scriptural Meditation

People get stuck because they can't see things from another angle or find a bigger pattern. It is only when someone really listens that others can help us look at things from a different point of view. What most people need is a good listening to, rather than a good talking to. When someone really listens to us we know it, we know we have been heard. At that point little miracles can happen. The other person sees into us from a different angle. They can show us things that we may have missed.

The two disciples trusted the stranger on their journey, shared their own disappointment, and were gifted with a new way of seeing. Their energy levels were transformed, and their direction in life was literally reversed. But they only realised this in retrospect. While they were talking they were focussed totally on the problem of the cross, without realising that the energy of the resurrection was already burning brightly inside them. This stranger, their companion, was looking at their experience from an infinite point of view. The point of view of a loving God who meets people in suffering. Realising that suffering might become a way to God was an amazing piece of news for the two disciples, and one that moved them deeper into their own journey of faith.

To live by faith is to see things always against an infinite horizon.

Ronald Rolheiser

Personal Reflection

Who has given you a good listening to?

How did it feel?

Prayer

Lord help me to be a good companion and a good listener on my journey through life. Help me to hear your pattern of dying and rising unfolding in my own life and the experience of those around me. Help me to hear your voice and hang on to hope, especially when things look black. Show me how to see things from your point of view. Make me a good listener so the seeds of resurrection might come to life in the experience of others.

AMEN

TURNING THE
HEART TO HOPE

The Fifth Station

The Breaking of Bread

Luke 24: 28 - 35

When they drew near to the village to which they were going, he made as if go on; but they pressed him to stay with them. 'It is nearly evening' they said 'the day is almost over.' So he went in to stay with them. Now while he was with them at table, he took the bread and said the blessing; then he broke it and handed it to them. And their eyes were opened and they recognised him; but he had vanished from their sight. Then they said to each other, 'Did not our hearts burn within us as he talked to us on the road and explained the scriptures to us?'

They set out that instant and returned to Jerusalem. There they found the eleven assembled together with their companions, who said to them, 'Yes, it is true. The Lord has risen and has appeared to Simon.' Then they told their story of what had happened on the road and how they had recognised him at the breaking of bread.'

Life Experience

I laughed my socks off when my husband John told me his new boss was a woman. I began to worry when he told me she was seven years younger than he was. I was petrified when he invited her round for a meal one evening. I felt like kicking him for only giving me a week's notice. I wanted to get a cleaning firm in and a catering firm to organise everything. I panicked.

When she arrived I knew I was on edge and I could see that she knew that too. We got through the first course of the meal politely enough, and then something changed between the three of us. A sense of peace seemed to settle around us and the conversation changed. I watched her as she talked and realised that this young face was furrowed with the lines of wisdom. I heard her talking about family struggles and health problems that I could never have coped with.

She was courageous in conversation but not over the top. She seemed to know herself. I realised that it was from her that the peace seemed to spill out all over the table. There seemed to be so many connections, common threads between her life and ours that we both found ourselves talking to her about our life together, about things we hadn't spoken of for years.

I was so wrapped up in the talk that John had to remind me that the main course was waiting. She left all too soon after the meal, but something remained. Since then John and I have been able to talk to each other in a different way. We can now talk about the difficult things we both face and keep them in perspective. As a result we've both been more cheerful too. It was just an ordinary meal but for both of us it was a major turning point in our lives.

Life
Experience

Scriptural Meditation

We sometimes think that when God breaks through into our lives he will appear surrounded by angels and heavenly music. In fact God often comes to us in the ordinary moments and is only recognised in retrospect. Jesus spent a lot of time in meals, in being sociable. He was courageous in conversation, and seemed to enjoy ordinary events, and be able to see through to deeper needs and potential. The ordinariness of the meal at Emmaus, at the end of a long walk, was the very place where Jesus let his risen presence be recognised. It is as if Jesus is challenging us to find him within our own relationships. The kingdom of God is among you, Jesus reminds us. In our friendships and in the people we work with. Sometimes, in breaking open the bread of our own lives in conversation, it seems that Jesus himself is there again, a hidden guest at our side. Those are the times when words can run out of meaning and a sacred silence settles on us. At other times it becomes that moment of recognition when we are challenged in faith, like the disciples, to say "It is the Lord".

The angels keep their ancient places; -
Turn but a stone, and start a wing!
'Tis ye, 'tis your estrangèd faces,
That miss the many-splendoured thing.

Francis Thompson

Personal Reflection

Can you recall any meals or conversations that you realise now were sacred?

Places where God has spoken to you?

Prayer

Lord of life, risen and present in every conversation and meal. Help us to recognise your presence in the wisdom and sincerity of others. Teach us to tune our hearts and minds to recognise your presence in conversation, sharing the ordinary moments of each day. Let your resurrection break through into the whole of our lives, and lead us to the fullness of life here in this world and forever.

AMEN

LIFE BREAKS IN

The Sixth Station

Jesus appears to his disciples

John 20: 19 –21

In the evening of that same day, the first day of the week, the doors were closed in the room where the disciples were, for fear of the Jews. Jesus came and stood among them. He said to them, ‘Peace be with you’, and showed them his hands and his side. The disciples were filled with joy when they saw the Lord, and he said to them again, ‘Peace be with you.’

Life Experience

I know it was stupid, but I felt so ashamed. Being a single mother is hard enough, but when your only son is arrested and locked up for violent crime, it is even harder. For three weeks I didn't even answer the door, and I did my shopping at an out-of-town supermarket. My family was two hours drive away, and I dare not even tell them about Brian's arrest. I heard the doorbell ring regularly, but I ignored it. I put the rubbish out late at night, and watched so much daytime TV that I nearly went mad. I slept late and woke late. I was falling apart.

I came down one morning. My brother was sat there, in my chair with a cup of coffee. To this day he won't tell me how he got into the house. At first I was shocked. Then I was angry with him. What right had he got to trespass into my space! I could have him arrested. Then I thought of my son's arrest and I slumped onto the settee and cried. I then realised that Alan, my brother, had moved. He was sitting beside me, on the settee, holding my hand.

He was exactly what I needed and exactly what I couldn't ask for. I had been locked in on myself, trapped by fear and isolated from life. He broke through my shame and disappointment. He reminded me that I still had a life to lead. He made me aware that my neighbours were worried, and that Brian needed his mother more than ever. His warmth and presence gave me the strength to do what I could not do alone.

The arrival of Alan was a resurrection moment after my painful few days. From that time on, peace and hope seeped back into my heart and I was able to accept the help of others and not be so independent and proud.

Life

Experience

Scriptural Meditation

The image of closed doors is one that we all know about. We sense the way people are closed, and know our own fear of being open and honest with others. Some people close themselves off from life by going quiet. Others close themselves off by talking so much that the real inside-story is well concealed. Others just keep so busy that the doors to their own heart are closed even from themselves. But it is in the heart, and in the shadowy parts of ourselves, that we meet the risen Jesus. He sets us free for new life. The disciples had good reason to be scared, they expected that the execution of Jesus might also happen to them. They were keeping quiet. But Jesus just walked through the doors they had locked bringing peace and life and new hope.

In daily experience we will find people and situations where peace, new life and hope suddenly break through. They are moments when the light of the resurrection shines through a good friendship or an honest word. They are probably more common than we think. As followers of a risen Lord there is a challenge for us to be signs of hope. We can help liberate others from their fear by an honest friendship and silent prayer that invites the risen Lord into every conversation.

The resurrection is not a doctrine we try to prove
Or a problem we argue about:
It is the life and action of Christ himself
In us by his Holy Spirit.

Thomas Merton

Personal Reflection

How do you lock yourself away from life and who can break through?

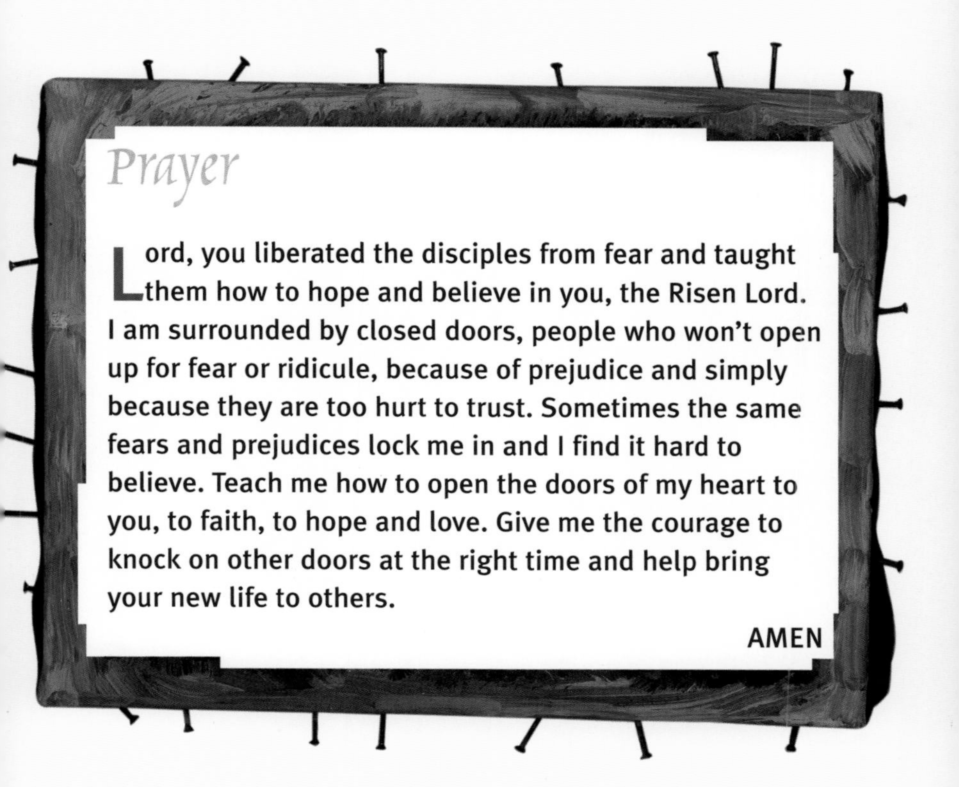

Prayer

Lord, you liberated the disciples from fear and taught them how to hope and believe in you, the Risen Lord. I am surrounded by closed doors, people who won't open up for fear or ridicule, because of prejudice and simply because they are too hurt to trust. Sometimes the same fears and prejudices lock me in and I find it hard to believe. Teach me how to open the doors of my heart to you, to faith, to hope and love. Give me the courage to knock on other doors at the right time and help bring your new life to others.

AMEN

NEW REASONS
FOR LIVING AND
HOPING

The Seventh Station

The Mission of the Apostles

John 20: 21 - 23

The disciples were filled with joy when they saw the Lord, and he said to them again, *'Peace be with you.*

'As the Father sent me,
So am I sending you.'

After saying this he breathed on them and said:

'Receive the Holy Spirit.
For those whose sins you forgive,
They are forgiven;
For those whose sins you retain,
They are retained.'

Life Experience

Our driver pushed the first-aid kit into my hands and shouted, "Get on with it!" I was the only one in the car who had done a first-aid course but I wasn't ready to face the road accident that lay ahead of us in the quiet country lane. I stumbled out of the car and along the ditch, avoiding the glass and debris on the road, my mind racing. I had completed the course two years ago after a spell in hospital. I'd had an accident at work and it made me realise how vital first aid was. I wanted to give something back after the help I had received. But that was two years ago. Now I couldn't remember a thing and was in a panic as I approached the car door.

I opened the door gently and looked at the driver. He was huddled over the wheel and was crying. There was no one else in the car. I leaned over and turned the engine off. Silence fell. I stopped and realised what I'd done. Without even thinking, I had done the right thing. Somehow I did remember and I realised I could cope. The training I had received two years ago was still there.

He turned and looked at me through the tears, and I noticed one shoulder was lower than the other. I asked him to stay still and started talking to him as I checked gently for other injuries. I heard my voice coming out calm and reassuring, as if it was someone else's voice. His shoulder was broken and he had probably crushed some ribs on his right side, but he was breathing well and could talk sensibly. As the paramedics arrived he turned to me and wanted to shake my hand.

I told him he'd better not with a broken shoulder. He just smiled and said, "You were sent from heaven. Thanks!"

When I returned to my friends, they slapped me on the back and said they knew I could manage. I was surprised by their confidence in me.

Life

Experience

Scriptural Meditation

When Jesus came into the room among his disciples it was a kind of graduation ceremony for them. They had accompanied him through all his work with people, with religious leaders, and the sick who came to him for help. They had spent time listening and talking together with Jesus, and had watched the process of arrest and execution before reaching the resurrection. Now Jesus invites them to do the same, to be sent into that pattern of dying and rising just as he was.

We too have experienced the presence of Jesus in our hearts, we have touched life and death in the small and large events of life, and have helped others along the road. We have touched life and so we are challenged to share life. To share our faith and our hope in resurrection.

In the footsteps of Jesus, we are asked to be signs and bearers of God's love. For some of us that might mean giving first-aid to those who have been hurt by life. For some of us it could mean being cheerful and optimistic when times are tough. For others it could mean opening up the wisdom at the heart of everyone, the wisdom that comes from God. Like a ripple, the resurrection should spread through us to a waiting world.

We have been called to share the resurrection of Christ
Not because we have fulfilled all the laws
Of God and mankind,
Not because we are religious heroes,
But because we are suffering and struggling human beings,
Sinners fighting for our lives
Prisoners fighting for our freedom
Rebels taking up spiritual weapons
Against powers that degrade
And insult our human dignity.

Thomas Merton

Personal Reflection

In what ways have I been a sign of hope and resurrection in the lives of others?

Prayer

Lord, help me to believe in resurrection as something that is happening now, not just when I die. Help me to see your life growing through laughter. In all the help and hope of relationships. Help me to find, in every situation, new reasons for living and hoping, so that the light of your resurrection can shine through my life and support others.

AMEN

TOUCHING
WOUNDS

The Eighth Station

Jesus confirms the faith of Thomas

John 20: 24 - 29

Thomas, called the Twin, who was one of the Twelve, was not with them when Jesus came. When the disciples said, 'We have seen the Lord,' he answered, 'Unless I see the holes that the nails made in his hands and can put my finger into the holes they made, and unless I can put my hand into his side, I refuse to believe.' Eight days later the disciples were in the house again and Thomas was with them. The doors were closed, but Jesus came in and stood among them. 'Peace be with you,' he said. Then he spoke to Thomas, 'Put your finger here; look, here are my hands. Give me your hand; put it into my side. Doubt no longer but believe.' Thomas replied, 'My Lord and my God!' Jesus said to him:

'You believe because you can see me.
Happy are those who have not seen and yet believe.'

Life Experience

It wasn't easy going to talk to someone. I was so confused and I hated to admit it. I like to be in control and understand everything, but my mind was a scrambled mix of bitterness and tears, and there was blackness there too that frightened me to death. Too much had happened to me; family deaths, a betrayal by a friend, the sack after a long illness, and still all the responsibility of a family to carry. I knew I was at breaking point.

I went for two sessions and told the sad story in full. I felt it helped but only a bit. But then something happened during the third visit. I got beyond saying what happened, to how I really felt inside. I came face to face with my own pain and anger. It seemed to be sweeping me away, so powerful was the emotion.

Then the counsellor simply said, "At last I can hear the real you." Beyond the facts, beyond consequences, she had sensed my personal pain, and it was such a relief to know that I could connect with someone at that level and be accepted. She helped me to find my wounds and touch them, and name them. In that shared acceptance there was a renewal of faith in life and hope for the future. It wasn't a pleasant process but it was life-giving.

It was a resurrection through the pain to a new level of love for others, and for myself too. I wouldn't want to go through it again, but I know it wasn't wasted. My pain was touched, and I was changed for the better.

Life Experience

Scriptural Meditation

Allowing someone to touch you where you are already hurt is a real act of faith. Yet Jesus comes to Thomas to allow him to do just that. Jesus is making an act of faith in Thomas and becoming vulnerable again. For Thomas the issue is different. It is as if Thomas needs to know that this is the same Jesus as he knew before, the one he had listened to and shared life with for three years. The only way he knew that he could not be deceived was by seeing the wounds, and touching them. By seeing the signs of the death he had witnessed, and yet touching someone who was alive, Thomas became convinced that, in Jesus, death itself had been overcome.

In touching what is painful in another person, we awaken the possibility of a deeper relationship of trust, and a more earthy appreciation of the mystery of life. God is to be found, not only in the high emotion of religion, but in the messy, sometimes violent, accidents and disappointments of life. He is the God who has lived through that kind of physical and psychological pain. He can then touch our wounds, look us in the eye and say, "I know".

God speaks to us with the authority of one who has suffered, and is with us on the journey that leads to resurrection. Like Thomas, we need to know that Jesus is with us in the darkness and suffering of our lives. It is only when we have the courage to let Jesus touch our wounds, that believing in resurrection takes on an earthy as well as eternal energy.

Christ lives in us
And leads us
Through mutual encounter and commitment
Into a new future
Which we build together for one another.
That future is called the Kingdom of God.

Thomas Merton

Personal Reflection

We all carry wounds, they are the price of wisdom, but how do you touch them?

How do you allow others to touch them?

Prayer

Lord, we are wounded people, and our wounds challenge us to be tender with what is broken in ourselves and in others. You did not crush the bruised reed or quench the wavering flame. Help me to be gentle with all that is bruised and broken in me, and in others. Let those wounds be touched and transformed into signs of resurrection by an earthy faith and the kind of compassion shown to Thomas.

AMEN

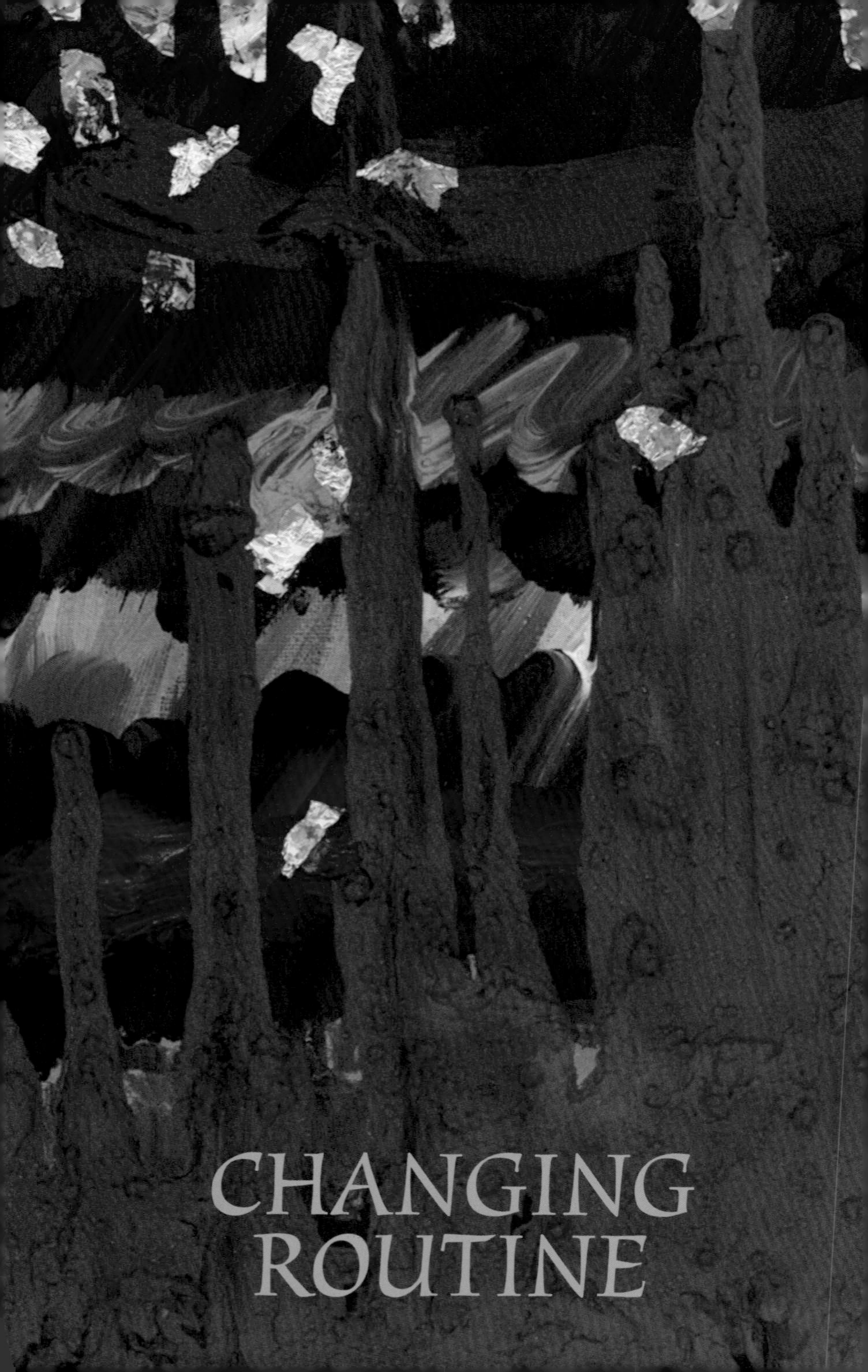
CHANGING
ROUTINE

The Ninth Station

By the Lake of Galilee

John 21: 1 – 10, 12 -14

Later on, Jesus showed himself again to the disciples. It was by the Sea of Tiberias, and it happened like this: Simon Peter, Thomas called the Twin, Nathanael from Cana in Galilee, the sons of Zebedee and two more of his disciples were together. Simon Peter said, 'I'm going fishing'. They replied, 'We'll come with you'. They went out and got into the boat but caught nothing that night.

It was light by now and there stood Jesus on the shore, though the disciples did not realise that it was Jesus. Jesus called out, 'Have you caught anything, friends?' And when they answered, 'No', he said, 'Throw the net out to starboard and you'll find something'. So they dropped the net, and there were so many fish that they could not haul it in. The disciple Jesus loved said to Peter, 'It is the Lord'. At these words, 'It is the Lord', Simon Peter, who had practically nothing on, wrapped his cloak round him and jumped into the water. The other disciples came on in the boat, towing the net and the fish; they were only about a hundred yards from land.

As soon as they came ashore they saw that there was some bread there, and a charcoal fire with fish cooking on it. Jesus said, 'Bring some of the fish you have just caught'. Jesus said to them, 'Come and have breakfast'. None of the disciples was bold enough to ask, 'Who are you?'; they knew quite well it was the Lord. Jesus then stepped forward, took the bread and gave it to them, and the same with the fish. This was the third time that Jesus showed himself to the disciples after rising from the dead.

Life Experience

As a police officer I need to live a disciplined life. In fact I like routine and organisation. One of my routines is to go for a jog through the park and then out around the golf course. I used to do it three or four times a week until recently. A month ago someone started taking pot-shots at me from one of the houses at the side of the park. After a few enquiries, it turned out that one of the characters I had locked up a few years ago had moved into one of the houses. They called him Arty but there was little that was beautiful about him. Nothing could be proved, but reluctantly I decided not to rock the boat and find a new jogging route.

I dug out a map of the area and looked at other possibilities, and eventually tried one out. It was good enough but there was too much road work, and I ran it with resentment.

That is until one Wednesday when I saw one of the admin staff from work in her jogging kit. I soon found I had a running companion who was more or less at my level. Within a week we were jogging together regularly and built up a friendship that was to prove vital as the stress of work got more difficult to cope with.

I enjoyed the company as much as the jogging and both did me so much good. I had never thought that I would find a friend through jogging. I wouldn't have if Arty had not messed up my routine and forced me to look at other alternatives.

Life

Experience

Scriptural Meditation

We all have many sorts of useful routines. They help us to get on with life as if we were on automatic pilot. Washing up, walking to work and even driving the car can be routines that ease us through the day. But they can also become blinkers that might block out new possibilities and new life. The disciples, on their boat, were on automatic pilot. They were experienced professionals slipping back into routine after the trauma of Jesus' death and resurrection. But the routine hadn't worked that night, and they were empty-handed until advice from a stranger changed their routine. Suddenly they realised that it was the Lord guiding them to a new way of working.

How many times has the Lord stood on the lake-shore of our lives and called out to us to do things differently? How many times have we heard the voice of a stranger go straight to our hearts? To recognise, like St John, that *It is the Lord!* The risen Jesus seems to slip through our lives and offer us new life in interruptions, coincidences and setbacks. This new offer of resurrection is always challenging us to look to a wider horizon. It is never a life that can be contained or tamed by plans and procedures. The risen life does not flow evenly, but follows the rhythm of a spirit that moves in mystery. Searching us out, even as we struggle towards it. It is a life that asks us to be open, and ready to move in new ways. We recognise the Lord, inviting us to meet him in ordinary moments like breakfast.

We must never
Let our religious ideas,
Customs, rituals, and conventions
Become more real to us
Than the risen Christ.

Thomas Merton

Personal Reflection

What routines or patterns of thinking seem to close you down and separate you from the presence of God?

Prayer

Lord of the risen life, thank you for the disruption that leads me to find you in new ways and different places. As life changes, show me how to change with it, and deepen my relationship with you. Keep my eyes open for you on the edges of my life, and give me the courage to trust the challenge of voices that seem strange to my way of thinking. Help me to use routine well, and not allow it to dull my senses to the surprising and disruptive side of your risen life.

AMEN

NEW STRENGTH
THROUGH
FRAILTY

The Tenth Station

Jesus confirms Peter as leader

John 21: 15 - 19

After the meal Jesus said to Simon Peter, 'Simon son of John, do you love me more than these others do?' He answered, 'Yes Lord, you know I love you.' Jesus said to him, 'Feed my lambs.' A second time he said to him, 'Simon son of John, do you love me?' He replied, 'Yes, Lord, you know I love you.' Jesus said to him, 'Look after my sheep'. Then he said to him a third time, 'Simon son of John, do you love me?' Peter was upset that he asked him the third time, 'Do you love me?' and said, 'Lord, you know everything; you know I love you'. Jesus said to him, 'Feed my sheep.

'I tell you most solemnly,
when you were young
you put on your own belt
and walked where you liked;
but when you grow old
you will stretch out your hands,
and somebody else will put a belt round you
and take you where you would rather not go.'

In these words he indicated the kind of death by which Peter would give glory to God.

Life Experience

I was sent home from work within an hour of arriving. The medical supervisor called it administrative leave. One of the nurses had smelt alcohol on my breath when I started my shift at the hospital, and reported me. The subsequent test proved positive. I got no sympathy and because of my senior-staff role I knew my job was over. This was the third time I'd done this, and the usual written warning was not going to be enough. I was supposed to be a leader, an example. Here I was, being reported by a junior and suspended. Then I had to face my family. The shame of it all left me sat on the wall outside the house in tears. What a mess, what a fool I'd been!

For three weeks I sat at home, watching the repeats of old films on daytime TV and feeling very sorry for myself and angry too. I loved my job, and now it had gone.

Then one evening my supervisor came around and sat down with me. He brought the nurse who had blown the whistle on me and they both put a proposition to me.

They knew that I was good at my job, but not disciplined enough. They wanted me back on the team, but things had to change. I was relieved but worried too. They wanted me to get help with my drink problem and join a group like Alcoholics Anonymous. They also wanted to run the shift on a team basis rather than have a manager like me. In effect it was demotion, I would have to deal with my problem, and work more with others. Yet it seemed to me that I would get my life back. Since then I have found it easier to admit my mistakes and be a bit less arrogant. I was lucky to get another chance and I took it with a grateful heart.

Life

Experience

Scriptural Meditation

Peter had a personal resurrection moment as he heard Jesus invite him back into the role of disciple. He knew that he had not stood up for Jesus after his arrest. He knew that he had lied about knowing him three times. Here Jesus wipes the slate clean by making him repeat his commitment three times in public. He forgives him, and re-instates him among the group of disciples. He must have been a chastened and humbler man after that exchange, reconciled but realistic about his strengths and weaknesses.

Meeting our own shortcomings sometimes seems like death, but as Jesus reminds us, the truth sets us free. Our relationship with the risen Jesus involves being grateful for gifts and strengths. As we grow older, the awareness of our fragility can lead to a deeper relationship with the mystery of resurrection. It is as if we meet the Risen Lord in the shadow of our lives. He is there to walk with us through failure and weakness, and help us rise again through wisdom and humility. The path to resurrection takes us all through the shadow side of life many times. There are no short cuts, no 'Star Trek' spaceship to beam us up and avoid problems. It is often in shame and setbacks that we learn to put our hand into the wounded hands of Jesus and trust the road of resurrection.

We rise to heaven on the stepping stones of our own failures.

Fr Harold Wrangham SDB

Personal Reflection

In what ways have setbacks and failures led you deeper into life and faith?

Prayer

Lord, we live in a culture that idolises success, and yet the path to resurrection always takes us through the shadow of death. It is only there, in the shadows of shame and weakness, that I can really allow you to be Lord and to redeem and transform what I am helpless to change. Help me to trust that you are with me in failure, as well as in success. Help me to realise that I am accepted in my frailty because it is the place where I am lifted up and set free for eternal friendship with God.

AMEN

BEING GOOD
NEWS

The Eleventh Station

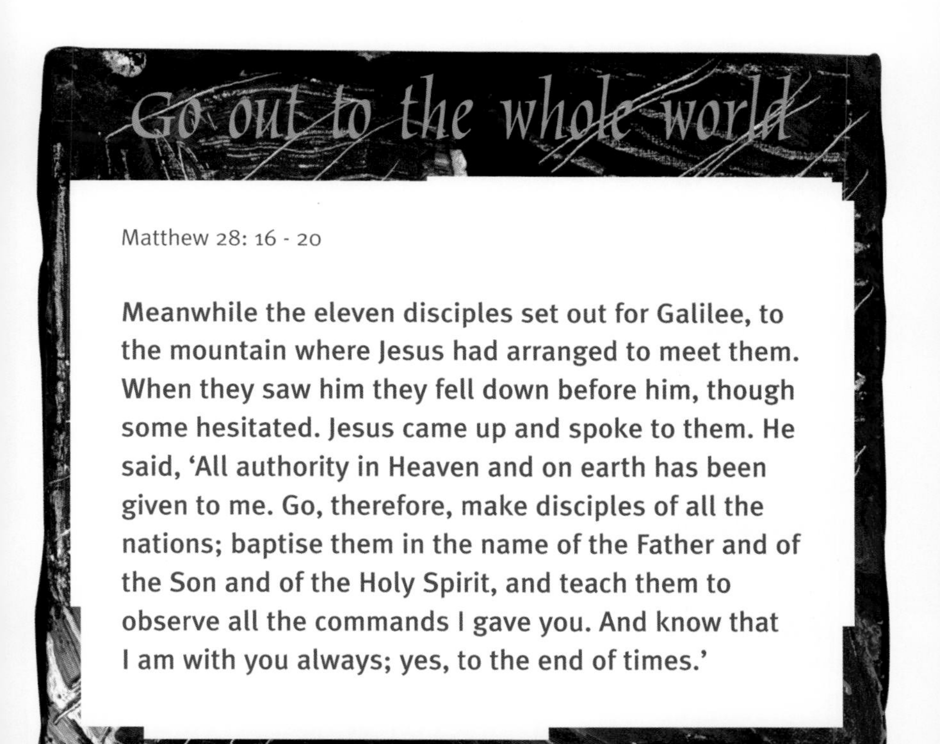

Matthew 28: 16 - 20

Meanwhile the eleven disciples set out for Galilee, to the mountain where Jesus had arranged to meet them. When they saw him they fell down before him, though some hesitated. Jesus came up and spoke to them. He said, 'All authority in Heaven and on earth has been given to me. Go, therefore, make disciples of all the nations; baptise them in the name of the Father and of the Son and of the Holy Spirit, and teach them to observe all the commands I gave you. And know that I am with you always; yes, to the end of times.'

Life Experience

I enjoy belonging to our local Residents Association. The chairperson, Maggie, is fair-minded and clear. The work is hard, but we get along together. I have learnt a lot and I felt comfortable about the whole thing, until last Wednesday. At our usual monthly review it turned out that Maggie couldn't make the presentation we'd promised at a national congress, and they had decided to send me!
I would have to speak to over 200 delegates on the work of our Association. I came out of the meeting in a daze, petrified at the thought of talking to so many clever and confident people. I found it hard enough to speak at the monthly meeting, but 200 strangers would leave me dumbstruck!

I grabbed Maggie straightaway, and said I couldn't do it and that she would need to send someone else. When she asked for reasons I found myself repeating that I just couldn't do it. "What you mean is that you are scared out of your wits," she said shrewdly.
I nodded. Maggie told me that it had been discussed at length last week, and that I was the best person to represent the association.

I had been there since the beginning, I knew the whole story, and I was a member of the local community. Before I could protest she continued, "And before you say otherwise we believe you have things to say which no one else can say. You have a feel for this Association which needs to be communicated." I gave in. I still needed a lot of help in organising myself and using a few pictures.

I did it even though some of the questions were a bit nasty! More surprisingly, I enjoyed the experience! When I said that later Maggie just smiled. It makes me mad when people sometimes know me better than I know myself!

Life

Experience

Scriptural Meditation

They say that good news travels fast. But the news of resurrection is so good that it is almost unbelievable and disturbing. St Mark describes the first reaction to resurrection in his Gospel as the women being *scared out of their wits*. (Mark 16: 8) The first reaction to new life and change is often uncertainty. Jesus knows that the news his disciples proclaim will disturb as well as encourage. The disciples have hardly come to terms with the resurrection before Jesus sends them out to share it with others. He is sending them out with an experience of resurrection, and a story to tell. In the end it is our own story and experience that carry the good news to others. It is the way we live that proclaims resurrection.

Whilst it is true that, as Christians, we have to carry our cross we must also roll away the stone from the tombs. We need to set free the energy of resurrection in the world around us. There are many things that block the growth of new life in the world to which we are sent; injustice, prejudice, violence and fear. These can trap us into tombs and leave the story of our lives unfinished. Jesus sends us out to share the experience of resurrection and set other people free, even though they may find it hard to accept.

We write a gospel every day
By the things we do and the words we say.
Other people read it, whether faithless or true.
So what is the gospel according to you?

Anonymous

Personal Reflection

In what ways do you feel you are good news to the world around you, a sign of resurrection and hope?

Prayer

Lord, help me to be cheerful and optimistic in my work and relationships. Help me to radiate that surprising hope that springs from the darkness and struggle of life. Show me how to challenge and change those who only proclaim prejudice and violence in their way of living. Give me a sense of eternal life in everything I do and help me to be a sign of new life to others, even when I know it may not always be welcome.

AMEN

SAYING GOODBYE

The Twelfth Station

Jesus Ascends

Acts 1: 9 - 11

As he said this he was lifted up while they looked on, and a cloud took him from their sight. They were still staring into the sky when suddenly two men in white were standing near them and they said, 'Why are you men from Galilee standing here looking into the sky? Jesus who has been taken up from you into heaven, this same Jesus will come back in the same way as you have seen him go there.'

Life Experience

The papers were beginning to take notice. We were making a difference to the way the asylum seekers were being looked after on our estate. It was hard but the action headquarters was buzzing and it was great to work with our MP on something we both felt passionate about. That afternoon was a highlight, we were having a press conference and the local news had just turned up to do some interviews. I loved the idea of being part of this, making a difference, standing side by side with Paul, our local Member of Parliament.

But standing behind the camera, watching Paul being interviewed, I was in for a shock. The presenter asked him a question about a cabinet reshuffle and he said that he had just been offered a ministerial post and was going to accept. "What will happen to the asylum campaign here?" a local reporter asked. Paul said he would keep in touch from a distance but that he had to leave it to others.

We were all very happy about his promotion but shocked and sad that he was leaving. What would we do? How would we handle the press, the links to local authorities and police without Paul? It seemed like the end, and yet Paul talked confidently about starting a grass-roots movement to stamp out prejudice across the nation.

Later that evening Paul spelt it out clearly for us. "The honeymoon is over," he said, "the future of this campaign depends upon hard work and commitment from the team. If I stay with you any longer I will just be holding back the hidden talent and the learning that needs to go on in the group." He told us that we would develop a stronger spirit in his absence. We went away that night a little sad and scared about the responsibility we faced and hoped he was right about the growth of a new spirit.

Life

Experience

Scriptural Meditation

There are times when we know that things are going too well to last. Great times, wonderful experiences, but you try hard not to get used to them. Like the autumn harvest that suddenly slips into a bitter winter, our lives roll through many seasons, none of which lasts forever. People and plans move through the same seasonal pattern and we are constantly challenged to say goodbye to one situation before we can embrace the new one. The disciples must have been confused and sad as they saw Jesus leave. They must have felt a kind of grief and emptiness. Their honeymoon was over and they were not sure what lay ahead.

Our lives unfold in a constant procession of hellos and goodbyes. People touch our lives, and leave us with an experience or a word. They move on along a path that may or may not cross our path again this side of the grave. Walking the way of resurrection does not mean avoiding these moments of loss, but taking a path through them to a deeper knowing of God in all things.

But (when so sad thou canst not sadder)
Cry - and upon thy so sore loss
Shall shine the traffic of Jacob's ladder
Pitched between Heaven and Charing Cross.

Francis Thompson

Personal Reflection

How do you deal with saying goodbye to familiar people and places?

Prayer

Lord, help me to keep moving forward on the way of resurrection. It is so easy to put my energy into the past, wishing that things had never changed. But to live is to change, and the way of resurrection calls us to change. Help me to think back to the past as a blessing, and a source of experience for the new challenges that lie ahead. Help me say my goodbyes with grace, and not cling to what will already have been kept safe in heaven.

AMEN

WAITING

The Thirteenth Station

Waiting for the Spirit

Acts 1: 12 - 14

So from the Mount of Olives, as it is called, they went back to Jerusalem, a short distance away, no more than a sabbath walk; and when they reached the city they went to the upper room where they were staying; there were Peter and John, James and Andrew, Philip and Thomas, Bartholomew and Matthew, James son of Alphaeus and Simon the Zealot, and Jude son of James. These joined in continuous prayer, together with several women, including Mary the mother of Jesus, and with his brothers.

Life Experience

"When are you going to settle down and get a proper job?" Alan could see the frustration on his Dad's face as he hid himself behind the evening paper. He did work and pay his way, but that wasn't good enough. His Dad wanted to see him settled with a career and some secure prospects, not working in cafés and doing voluntary work. The problem was Alan didn't know what he wanted. He listened to advice, looked at the career material in the library, but nothing moved him. There was nothing that set him on fire.

He told himself that when the right thing came along he would know it. But he wasn't really sure. He lay on his bed night after night listening to music, and thinking about what was important to him, what he was good at and if there was a place for him in this world. His Gran was great. She said, "When God made time, he made plenty of it". She encouraged him to wait and see.

So he did. Up in his room he thought about the conversations he listened to in the café. He remembered the fun he had shared working with the kids at the children's home. What could he do with his average exam results?

Then one night it was as if lightning struck him. He had heard how often people in the café complained about kids and how they ought to be locked up and controlled.

And he thought about the relaxed way he could work with difficult children, as a volunteer in the local community home. It had been staring him in the face all the time and his exam results would get him into some basic career training. It seemed so neat and so obvious now. There seemed to be a hundred different things dropping into place and he had the energy to cope with them. He felt a huge sense of gratitude and was glad he had waited for the penny to drop. He got dressed and went out to celebrate!

Life

Experience

Scriptural Meditation

We spend a lot of time waiting. We wait for a bus, for the telephone to ring, for an apology, for an exam result, for everything that is really valuable. The men and women in the upper room had to wait. They did not know what to do next. Neither did they have the energy to do anything. Like the sediment in a turbulent river, they needed to be still and let life settle before they could see clearly what God was asking of them. Like a surfer waiting in the water, they needed to hope for a wave that would move them forward toward the shore.

Our culture sometimes pushes people into action before the time is right, before the way is clear and the spirit has grown. Sometimes we are too busy making our plans to sense the plans and rhythm of God's life. When we look at life everything that is really valuable is waited for, the birth of a baby, the touch of love, maturity, wisdom, new energy and deep peace. All of these things are gifts from a God who asks us to trust and live a rhythm of action and reflective waiting on the way to resurrection.

Ideas need time and space
One idea will awaken others
Old ideas will influence new plans
Don't force the pace
Don't push the river.

Moving On

Personal Reflection

Recall a time when you had to wait for something important.

Reflect on how you felt about God at that time.

Prayer

Lord of time, I live my life according to the clock, appointments, television programmes, and meal times. So much of the day involves waiting for things to happen that are beyond my control. Help me to use those moments to deepen my trust in you and find a rhythm of relaxed reflection. Teach me not to be afraid of the empty spaces in my life.

AMEN

TOUCHED BY
FIRE

The Fourteenth Station

The Coming of the Spirit

Acts 2: 1 - 4

When Pentecost day came round, they had all met in one room, when suddenly they heard what sounded like a powerful wind from heaven, the noise of which filled the entire house in which they were sitting; and something appeared to them that seemed like tongues of fire; these separated and came to rest on the head of each of them. They were all filled with the Holy Spirit and began to speak foreign languages as the Spirit gave them the gift of speech.

Life Experience

I was about six years old, learning to ride a bike with my Dad. We had taken the balance wheels off the back and my Dad was holding the saddle as I pedalled down the quiet road. I kept looking back to get the reassurance of my Dad's smile as we moved along. "I think I'm getting the hang of it," I said over my shoulder. There was no reply. Suddenly I knew I was on my own, but I dare not look back for fear of falling off.

Somehow all the balance and awareness that had come from my Dad had been switched on inside me. I could do it! I was in touch with something in myself that was correcting, guiding and balancing me. I felt as if I had grown up and I was flying along the road under my own steam!

I should never have looked back or tried to wave to my Dad though, the next minute I was in a heap in the gutter. But I could do it! I knew there was something in me, some skill, some gift. The bruises and bent mudguard didn't matter. Somehow I had come alive from the inside. After weeks and weeks of struggle it had just happened!

Life

Experience

Scriptural Meditation

There are many moments, scattered through our lives, when we come alive. We grow in awareness, and suddenly see something that was always there in a totally new way. Like a jigsaw puzzle suddenly falling into place we understand how things fit together and the meaning behind apparently different events that make up our story. That sudden insight is rare for an individual, but even more amazing when it happens for a whole group. The men and women in the upper room spent their time waiting, reflecting and in silence. All of a sudden they received inspiration as a group. They were overcome with the joy and energy of insight and wisdom. They would never see the events of Jesus' life in the same way again. Jesus' life had become a revelation to them.

The miracle of that experience is that it happened instantaneously to the whole group. It left them free and ready to take up the path of resurrection that Jesus opened up for us all. Like the Berlin wall, all their confusion crumbled. The way ahead became clear for the whole group. The power of the experience was able to cut through differences of language and old prejudices. They were offered new hope and a new vision of a world heading towards eternal life and light, *the Via Lucis.*

Each of us will find moments of insight and inspiration on our own journey. Like finding a signpost when lost, it gives us hope and energy to keep moving forward. The inspiration of the Spirit also draws us together on a common journey as a church. A journey that awakens in others the presence of the Risen Lord, walking the road with us each day.

Communities are brought into being by men and women responding to a divine impulse towards society and relationship, the impulse to love and be loved, implanted by God who created them.

The Common Good 18

Personal Reflection

Recall a moment of inspiration in the ordinary experience of life.

How did it feel?

Where did it come from?

Prayer

Lord of creativity, stay with us when we are lost and waiting. Give us time to let the deadness of the past slip away from us, and help us to see the way ahead to new patterns and possibilities. May the path of your resurrection continue to unfold in these times. Help us to be aware of your Spirit nudging us and annoying us into action. May we play our part in bringing the light of resurrection into the sometimes confusing pattern of plans and relationships in our world.

AMEN

CROSS REFERENCE FOR LITURGICAL PREPARATION

	Via Lucis Station	Scripture Reference	Catholic Lectionary	Revised Common Lectionary
1	Jesus is Risen	Luke 24: 1 - 9	Easter Vigil (3)	
2	Peter and the other disciple run to the tomb	John 20: 3 - 9	Easter Day (ABC)	Easter Day (ABC)
3	Jesus appears to Mary of Magdala	John 20: 11-18		Easter Day (ABC)
4	On the road to Emmaus	Luke 24: 13 - 27	3rd Sunday Easter	Easter Day Evening 3rd of Easter(A)
5	The Breaking of Bread	Luke 24: 28 - 35	3rd Sunday Easter(1+2)	Easter Day Evening (ABC)
6	Jesus appears to his disciples	John 20: 19 –21		3rd of Easter (B)
7	The Mission of the Apostles	John 20: 21-23	2nd Sunday Easter Pentecost Sunday	2nd of Easter (ABC)
8	Jesus confirms the faith of Thomas	John 20: 24-29	2nd Sunday Easter	2nd Easter (ABC)
9	By the Lake of Galilee	John 21: 1-14	3rd Sunday Easter (3)	3rd Easter – Year C
10	Jesus confirms Peter as leader	John 21: 15-18	3rd Sunday Easter (3)	
11	Go out to the whole world	Mark 16: 15-18	Ascension (2)	
12	Jesus Ascends	Acts 1: 9-11	Ascension	Ascension (ABC) 7th of Easter (A)
13	Waiting for the Spirit	Acts 1: 12-14	7th Sunday Easter (1)	
14	The Coming of the Spirit	Acts 2: 1-42	Pentecost Sunday	Pentecost (ABC) 2nd Easter (A) 3rd Easter (A)

A Group Liturgy

Setting

A table is prepared with a principal candle, small candles for each person present, the book of the Gospels, and some flowers.
(In informal family settings some food and wine might be added).
The lighting should be subdued so that the candle can become the main focus.

Introduction

The Leader of the liturgy or the Head of the family should initiate the liturgy with the following or similar prayer.

To light candles in this room
Is to remind us
That Jesus is risen.
Whatever darkness fills our lives
His light has already overcome it.

To light this Easter candle
Is to connect us again
To the mystery of the risen Jesus
Alive and transforming
Each of our lives here today.

Prayer

Lord help us to see the light of your resurrection
Shining in each of our lives,
And strengthen our trust in you.

The Candle:

One of the group then lights the principal candle in silence.

The Gospel for the selected station on Via Lucis is read.

Quiet music is played for a few minutes or a period of silence.

Reading:

The leader then reads the reflection and/or the story.

Shared Reflection:

The group is invited to reflect in silence or share briefly their response to the question in the personal reflection
and then light one of the candles around the principal candle.

The prayer from the appropriate station is spoken by the leader.

Ending:

Some appropriate final song is sung or played.

Celebration:

A social time or meal is shared.

Possible Music For Group Liturgies

Theme	Title	Artist	Album	Reference
Gratitude/Optimism	Grateful	Art Garfunkel	Across America	Virgin Records VTCD113724384265526
Lead us to Light	The Prayer	Andrea Bocelli + Celine Dion	Sogno	Polydor PY 811
Uncertainty	Crossroads	Don McLean	American Pie	EMI CDP7 465552
Trusting the journey	Wherever the road goes	Heather Small	Proud	BMG 74321 765482
Presence on the journey	Ease your troubled mind	Heather Small	Proud	BMG 74321 765482
Perseverance	Holding on	Heather Small	Proud	BMG 74321 765482
	Pilgrim	ENYA	A day without rain	Warner 875385986-2
Deeper awareness	Love is the seventh wave	Sting	Best of Sting	A+M 540 3212
Coming out of the tomb	Desperado	Eagles	Very Best of The Eagles	Warner 9548 32375-2
Making the journey	Journey	911	911 The greatest Hits	Virgin 289972438 4855423
Home towards the light	I'll find my way home	Jon and Vangelis	The Best of Jon and Vangelis	Polydor 821929-4
Joy in Following Christ	Joy in The Journey	Michael Card	The Life	Sparrow SPC 1171-2